NO PAROLE TODAY

NO PAROLE TODAY

Laura Tohe

West End Press

Some of these poems have previously appeared in the following periodicals, journals, and collections: *AZ Native Scene; Blue Dawn, Red Earth; Blue Mesa Review; Braided Lives; Les Cahiers* (France); *Callaloo; Calyx; The Clouds Through This Light; Communicating Prejudice; The Daily Nebraskan; Estuaires Revue Culturelle* (Luxembourg); *Fever Dreams; Journal of Navajo Education; Laurus; Nebraska English Journal; The New Skyline Edition* (Germany); *Poetes Indiens D'Amerique* (France); *Scott Foresman Reader; Songs From This Earth on Turtle's Back; Wanbli Ho.*

Author acknowledgments: special gratitude to Simon Ortiz for his advice and editorial support, to Paul Olson whose support sustained me throughout, and to Deborah Plant and Mike Carroll who entered this process with the gift of friendship that nurtured the completion of this work. *A'héhee'.*

Fourth printing, August 2005
ISBN: 0-931122-93-7

Book design by Nancy Woodard
Front cover photos: "Names on Brick Wall at Indian School" and "Faces at Indian School, 1968–70" by Laura Tohe.

The Navajo font used to print this work is available from Linguist's Software, Inc. P.O. Box 580, Edmonds, WA 98020-0580.

West End Press • P.O. Box 27334 • Albuquerque, NM 87125

This book is dedicated to Laura Florence, to the memories of Julia T. Barton and Benson Tohe, and to all those who survived Indian schools everywhere.

Contents

Introduction

In Indian civilization I am a Baptist, because I believe in immersing the Indians in our civilization, and when we get them under holding them there until they are thoroughly soaked.—Richard Henry Pratt, Brigadier General of the United States Army, addressing the World Baptist Convention, 1883

Dear General Pratt,

Your address to the World Baptist Convention in 1883 binds you to the colonialist efforts of the Indian schools you instituted. While American history portrays you as a well-intentioned administrator of Indian education, the legacy that you founded would ultimately work to devastate the indigenous cultures of this country. The assimilation policies you put in place to turn Indian people into *civilized* white American citizens, who would dress, worship, think, and hold the values of the dominant culture, still affect us today.

I am a survivor, as my parents' and grandparents' generations were, of the legacy you established. Generations of Indian people spent *time* in these schools. In fact, my great-grandfather, Hoskie Thompson, was one of the first Diné students to attend Carlisle Institute. Living in boarding schools was similar to serving a sentence. We are veterans of these institutions. While some of us survived these schools, others ran away or died trying. Some died from loneliness or from a broken heart. A cemetery adjoined almost every Indian school.

During my grandmother's generation, she tasted food alien to her palate. On her way to boarding school, she tasted cheese for the first time. After biting into a cheese sandwich, she preferred to go hungry.

At the Indian school, my life was measured and accounted for on a daily basis: roll call, nine-week work details, lights out at ten p.m., lights on at five a.m. Fences surrounded my life. Cement covered the earth beneath my feet. In first through third grade, I marched to my classroom with a John Philip Sousa march playing over the intercom, which was, of course, apropos because you modeled Indian schools after the rigid military life in which you made a career. I can still identify a Sousa march even though I don't know its name.

Later I lived in the city at a government boarding school institution separated from my family and homeland. This separation was intended to further enable assimilation. Assimilation made us feel ashamed for what we were, where we came from, how we spoke, our stories, our families, how we dressed, and for speaking our language. Some well-intentioned parents even prohibited their children from speaking *Diné bizaad* at home to ensure their children's chances of "success in the white man's world."

The most crippling legacy of boarding schools is the devastation of our native languages and culture. We are still trying to recover from that loss. Separation from home, land, and culture equals loss of identity and language. Result: via contemporary urban Indian standards, a culture yardstick proves *Indianness*, whatever that is. The culture police may have an idea of what constitutes an *Indian* identity. It's kosher to be Indian nowadays. I doubt my parents and grandparents ever knew that, because they lived their lives according to the beliefs that were passed on to them void of the politics of being Indian. But being Indian now means having to prove our identity to other Indians, institutions, and the government especially. It's ironic how the government now funds Indian nations to help preserve and revitalize the languages you tried so vehemently to stamp out.

In the late 1950s I began school on the largest reservation in the United States, the Diné reservation. Although outsiders gave us the name Navajo, we call ourselves Diné, *The People*. I prefer to call myself the name my ancestor gave us because I am trying to de-colonize myself. When I began school, the Principal placed me in first grade because I was one of the few students who could speak English, though *Diné bizaad* was my mother tongue. All my classmates were Diné and most of them spoke little or no English.

On the first day of school we found ourselves behind small wooden desks looking at the teacher who acted on behalf of your assimilation policies. Besides teaching us to read, write, and count in English, she was instructed to wipe out *Diné bizaad* through shame and punishment. We still bear painful memories for speaking our native language in school and that legacy is partly why many indigenous people don't know their ancestral language.

I skipped Beginner class and went straight to First grade. My grandmother called me *hwiní'yu,* being useful, because I translated for my classmates. I felt their helplessness when English sounds couldn't form into language that would save them. If I didn't help them, I felt I would be a participant in their punishment. We learned quickly that if we didn't want to be punished and shamed in front of our classmates we had best speak our language in private, far from the ears of the teachers, or stop speaking; most chose the latter.

Ironically, the Diné language was successfully utilized as a secret code during World War II. Without the Code Talkers, the war might have had a substantially different outcome for America.

Because I spoke two languages, reading came easy for me. The repetitiveness of "Oh, oh, oh, see Sally jump, see Dick run," in the Dick and Jane series quickly bored me and I wanted to move on to more challenging reading. I became a reading tutor for my peers. Later my mother took me to a library where I checked out as many books as I could, and I read them all.

In school we never read about Indian people except during Thanksgiving, when we learned that *friendly* Indians showed the Pilgrims how to plant corn using fish as fertilizer, and that they brought a turkey slung over their shoulder (a stereotypical image) to the first Thanksgiving. Those Indians didn't dress like Diné, but we identified and were proud of them because they were dark-skinned, knew how to hunt, and shared food with the Pilgrims who nearly perished when they first arrived after escaping European oppression. We weren't ashamed to be Indians in school once a year, on Thanksgiving.

A hundred years after you made your statement to the Baptists, we are still here. We have not vanished, gone away quietly into the sunset, or assimilated into mainstream culture the way you envisioned. At least some of us haven't. Those who chose assimilation we call apples—red on the outside, white on the inside.

Your ideology conflicts with our fundamental beliefs about our relationship to each other, to the earth, and to the natural world. We come to this knowledge through the beliefs and teachings of our elders. We are who we are. Western culture has always been destructive to indigenous peoples and to the earth everywhere. You and your followers are still children who have not yet learned how to get along with each other or how to live in this world. Perhaps you are originally from another universe, as some of your intellectuals have asserted.

We are nearing the end of the twentieth century, and we continue to survive with the strength of the spirit of our ancestors. Our grandmothers and grandfathers taught us to hold to our beliefs, religions, and languages. That is the way of survival for us. Though we are still less than one percent of the U.S. population, Indian nations are growing. The Diné are the largest nation, and I say it is because we like to make love, not war—though we've fought wars too. Indigenous nations are probably the only Americans that resisted becoming *American*.

Your quotation, "Kill the Indian, save the man," binds you to the attitudes that were already in place in your time, attitudes that would subject Indian people to cultural genocide. People of your time speculated on what to do with *the Indian problem*. In the end there are no winners; there are only the victims and the survivors of an inhumane system, whether they are the colonizer or the decolonized.

I voice this letter to you now because I speak for me, no longer invisible, and no longer relegated to the quiet margins of American culture, my tongue silenced. The land, the Diné, the Diné culture is how I define myself and my writing. That part of my identity was never drowned; it was never a hindrance but a strength. To write is powerful and even dangerous. To have no stories is to be an empty person. Writing is a way for me to claim my voice, my heritage, my stories, my culture, my people, and my history.

Prologue: Once You Were Signed Up

A few years before her death my grandmother, Julia Barton,
narrated this story about her years at boarding school. She tells it
in Diné storytelling fashion, often ignoring time considerations.

I was three and a half then. I couldn't even reach the sink to turn on the water. The older girls took care of me. They lifted me up so I could wash my hands. I wore a denim-striped dress, white and blue. It went down to my ankles, black stockings and high-topped shsoes. All the kids wore this. Those were our uniforms. They lined us up and we learned to march like soldiers. We even learned the calls. They told us to walk and sit up straight.

My mother came to see me, but not very often. It was quite a long ways on horseback. They had to come by horseback, you see, because back then they didn't have cars or trucks. And there were only dirt roads. She stayed at St. Michaels where the priests were good to her. They brought us mutton, corn and bread. You know those blue corn cakes? We were always glad to get extra food. That's what the parents would bring us kids.

You know back then we couldn't go home anytime. They made you stay once you got there. You had to stay the whole year. Once you were signed up, you just had to tough it out. There was this janitor who used to tell us the news about the war and the soldiers. We used to like to hear about it, how our soldiers were doing. Maybe a few of our people were there. We learned how to fold the flag.

I stayed in Fort Defiance till I was in the fifth grade. Then I wanted to go to Sherman Institute in California because that's where my aunt was. She had a job in Los Angeles cleaning houses. She was one of the first ones to go. She wanted me to come and I even asked to go down there. But instead they sent me to Haskell in Kansas. We got on the train in Gallup and that was the first time I ever rode a train.

In the morning it was green and so pretty outside. They gave us cheese sandwiches but we didn't eat them. We never ate cheese before. It rained all that time and then it got hot and stayed that way. We got to school standing up in an old truck. They assigned us our beds, where to work and go to school. Many more Indians were there: Cherokees, Choctaws, Blackfeet. Some had it worse than others. "Don't speak Indian," they told us. We got demerits if we did, no movies, extra work, work, work. We wore uniforms and shoes made by nameless prisoners. Always it was work, work, work.

I remember I had this friend; she was Osage. One time she said, "I want to show you something. I'm going to ask them for the key so I can get something out of my suitcase." We went down below into the basement. I was very young then. There were two girls in there already, in that dungeon, and it was a real dark place. The rooms were about from here to here, two of them. One on this side and one on that side. They had windows just on this side with little tiny holes. It was a metal place and it had just holes, just full of holes. That's the only window they had. Both sides just like that. There was just one bed with a mattress on it and one blanket. She whispered, "Come here." I was scared because it was dark. They had a light bulb, just barely enough to see. They didn't have a toilet but a bucket. They had a bucket down there for them. These two girls used to yell at night. We used to hear them yelling and crying. They were from Mount Taylor. They took off with the boys and tried to run away. They must've been about seventeen or eighteen years old. They usually stayed about a month down there, a whole month.

The boy's jail was right in front of the school house. The jail was that big. The back part was okay but the front part it had *ha'á't'íída,* whatchamacallit bars. *Áko,* so that we used to see who was in jail there as we went into the classroom. *Hágoshii aadéé̜' naazį́į̜le áshiiké',* the boys used to stand in there. They had their own jail. *Nihi éí,* we had those dungeons down there. The boys had the open jail outside. The front part would be open, with bars. But I guess at night they closed it. During the day we used to see who was in jail as we went into the classroom. They wouldn't let us visit them. At that time they wouldn't even let you look at your boyfriend. You couldn't even speak to them. The boys in jail would call you or they'd say, "I'm so and so." They would yell but we weren't supposed to talk to them.

We had military rules and we had to learn the commands. You had to get in line in the morning. We were marched everywhere we went, classrooms, dining room, church, everywhere. We even had chaperones to follow us to the classroom. In the morning we lined up and we'd go outside. The flag had to be raised. We all had to salute military-like.

Some of us ran away and were caught. They balled and chained us just like in those old silent movies. We never wrote home; there was nobody to read English because we were all in school. If we wanted to go home, they told us we'd have to pay our own way. Of course, our families didn't have much money. So we stayed for four years and never went home.

Later, when I got back to Fort Defiance, that sickness, that real bad sickness came on, German measles. They said the soldiers brought it back from Germany. And so it spread through the schools and our school was hit real hard. Everybody was in bed. St. Michaels closed, and they sent the Sisters from there to Fort Defiance to help.

At first a lot of us didn't mind. They told us not to go in the rooms where the sick ones were. The doors were closed. But, you know, you get sick overnight. That's how I got sick. I was all right the night before. Here the next day I couldn't stand. I was so sick I wanted to vomit. I was aching all over. My whole body was aching. Then they put us upstairs. They put me up there too. Those that they didn't expect to live very long were put upstairs. Your great-grandmother who was there at the time said I was real sick. Somehow she sent word back home. My mother tried to get in there. We were quarantined and nobody could get in. They had policemen down at the trading post keeping everyone away. They weren't letting anybody in. They fed us just soup and crackers. I guess we were in bed about two months. We got soup and bread that was hard as a rock. I saw a lot of my friends die. They covered them up with sheets. The men came and took the bodies out. They threw the mattresses out the window. Then they replaced them and put someone else on them. Lucky some of us didn't go. Some others just died. I watched them die. They got nosebleeds and vomited at the same time. There was nobody around to help. You couldn't get up to help because you were so weak yourself. The only ones that didn't get sick were the Sisters. I don't know why they didn't. It was a very bad time.

We made sock balls. We unraveled socks and made balls. We used to darn socks for the boys and we'd unravel the worst ones and put rubber bands inside it to make a ball. We used to keep bumblebees for pets. We'd tie a string around it and tie it somewhere outside. After school we'd go back and find it. Then we'd untie it and let it fly around. We had lots of fun play—ing with our bumblebee pets.

We had a playground and a merry-go-round that would take you up, way up as high as this house. If you did it right, if you could hold on, you would go way up. Boy, we used to stick. We used to dare each other, "I'll bet you can't do it." We'd get up on the slide and slide down those great big poles and we'd chase each other around.

At Fort Defiance they took us out for walks on Sundays if the weather was good. I don't know why we used to like to go to the graveyard. The matrons used to ask us, "Where do you want to go for a walk?" "Graveyard!"

We weren't even afraid of the *ch'íídiis,* ghosts. I guess it was the only place we didn't get scolded. We used to read all those little plates, you know, that say so and so is buried here, and then we'd ask to go down to Red Lake where the water flows down. Well, we went down to that wash and we'd take our shoes off and walk in there. Then we'd come back down and go back over the hill to school. We never ran off.

I got back at the end of my third year from Haskell because the doctor said I needed a drier climate. It was good to get back as we drove along in that old rickety truck that kept breaking down. It was good to get home, good to see my mother and all the ones at home. It was good to be home.

Part I

Kill the Indian, Save the Man
—Richard Henry Pratt

Our Tongues Slapped into Silence

In first grade I was five years old, the youngest and smallest in my class, always the one in front at group picture time. The principal put me in first grade because I spoke both Diné and English. Because of that, I skipped Beginner class.

All my classmates were Diné and most of them spoke only the language of our ancestors. During this time, the government's policy meant to assimilate us into the white way of life. We had no choice in the matter; we had to comply. The taking of our language was a priority.

Dick and Jane Subdue the Diné

> *See Father.*
> *See Mother.*
> *See Dick run.*
> *See Jane and Sally laugh.*
>   *oh, oh, oh*
> *See Spot jump.*
>   *oh, oh, oh*
> *See Eugene speak Diné.*
> *See Juanita answer him.*
>   *oh, oh, oh*
> *See teacher frown.*
>   *uh oh, uh oh*

In first grade our first introduction to Indian School was Miss Rolands, a black woman from Texas, who treated us the way her people had been treated by white people. Later I learned how difficult it was for black teachers to find jobs in their communities, so they took jobs with the Bureau of Indian Affairs in New Mexico and Arizona in the 1950s and 60s.

Miss Rolands found it difficult to adjust to living in a mostly Diné community, connected to the outside world by only a dirt road that was sometimes impassable in the winter.

> *See Eugene with red hands, shape of ruler.*
>   *oh, oh, oh*

See Eugene cry.
    oh, oh, oh
See Juanita stand in corner, see tears fall down face.

    oh, oh, oh

In first grade we received the first of our Dick and Jane books that introduced us to the white man's world through Father, Mother, Dick, Jane, Puff and Spot. These and other characters said and did what we thought all white people did: drive cars to the farm, drain maple juice from trees, and say oh, oh, oh a lot.

Oh see us draw pictures
    of brown horses under blue clouds.
We color eyes black, hair black.
We draw ears and leave out mouth.

    Oh see, see, see, see.

Miss Rolands, an alien in our world, stood us in the corner of the classroom or outside in the hallway to feel shame for the crime of speaking Diné. Other times our hands were imprinted with red slaps from the ruler. In later classes we headed straight for the rear of classrooms, never asked questions, and never raised our hand. Utter one word of Diné and the government made sure our tongues were drowned in the murky waters of assimilation.

The Names

Lou Hon, Suzie, Cherry, Doughnut, Woody, Wabbit, Jackie,
Rena Mae, Zonnie, Sena, Verna, Grace, Seline, Carilene

"Virginia Spears," the Algebra teacher calls roll
(Her name is Speans)
And Virgie winces and raises her hand.
"Here." Soft voice.
          She never corrects the teachers.

"Leonard T-sosie."
(His name is Tsosie.) Silent first letter as in ptomaine,
Ptolemy.
Silent as in never asking questions.
Another hand from the back goes up. No voice.

"Mary Lou Yazzy. Are you related to Thomas Yazzy?"
Yazzie is a common Navajo name, like Smith or Jones.
She rhymes it with jazzy and snazzy.
Mary Lou with puzzled expression. "No."
"Oh, I thought you might be. He's quiet too."

I start to tense up because I'm next
with my name that sticks out
like her sensible black high heeled lace-ups,
clap, clap, clap down the hall.
"Laura Toe."
And I start to sink,
to dread hearing it on the bus tossed around
          like kids playing keep-away.

Suddenly we are immigrants,
          waiting for the names that obliterate the past.

4

Tohe, from T'óhii means Towards Water.
Tsosie. Ts'ósí means Slender.
And Yazzie, from Yázhí, means Beloved Little One/Son.

The teacher closes the book and
we are little checkmarks besides our names.

Roanhorse, Fasthorse, Bluehorse, Yellowhorse, Begay, Deswod, Niilwod,
Chee, 'Átsidí, Tapahonso, Háábaah, Hastiin Nééz.

Cat or Stomp

to all the former cats and stomps
of the Diné Nation

The first few days back at the Indian School
        after summer vacation
you wore your new clothes wrangler tight jeans
        stitched on the side
and boots (if you were lucky enough to have a pair)
Tony Lama
Nacona
or Acme
a true stomp listened to country western music
        Waylon and George Jones
dying cowboy music and all that stuff

you wore
go go boots and bell bottoms if you were a cat
        and danced to the Rolling Stones
even if you wore tennis shoes it was clear which side
        you were on
Every year the smoking greyhound buses pulled up
        in front of the old
gymnasium bringing loads of students
fresh off the reservation dragging metal trunks,
        train cases and
cardboard boxes precariously tied with string
the word spread quickly
of some new kid from Chinle or Many Farms
"Is he a cat or stomp?" someone would ask
"Stomp"
and those with appropriate clothing
        would get their chance
                                    to dance with him that night

She's Real Quiet, a Letter from the Indian School I

Met this girl, Mae Jean from Saint Michaels. She's real quiet. Nobody gives her a hard time. None of the Mustangs, the girl gang, have it in for her. The matrons don't put her on extra detail like waxing and polishing the hallways or cleaning toilets. She's never on extra detail. She's real shy.

Mae Jean gets up early soon after the 5:30 lights come on. She showers, dresses, and styles her hair carefully into a puffy bouffant resembling a small tumbleweed. Every hair in place. At the beginning of school when we have money and supplies, she sprays a sticky mist of Aqua Net over her hair. If you watch her doing her hair, she gets embarrassed and drops her comb into the drawer and says she's ready.

She signed my yearbook with letters lined up perfectly on an invisible line. "To a real 'kool' chick I have known for the past years. It has been more than a pleasure knowing you and taking your jokes. I appreciate your kindness and friendship you have shown me; I will never forget it. Good luck toward your educational goals and may many happiness come your way in the years to come. Always, Mae Jean Begay A.H.S. '70."

On our way to the dining room this morning she tells me she's been here nine years, ever since she was six years old, longer than most of us. Nobody ever comes to visit her and she never goes home during vacations, not even Christmas. Doesn't have a boyfriend like some of the other girls. Never seen her drink, sniff glue or gasoline. Never gossips about the matrons and she doesn't cuss. She's Catholic but hardly ever goes to church. One time we went to the Presbyterian church just to have Oreo cookies and coffee because we missed breakfast. She's real quiet and calm. Laughs softly. She gets along with everybody. She's been here the longest of all of us. Mae Jean knows all the dos and don'ts at Indian school. Watch her.

Joe Babes

Joe Babes, the ones named
Jolene, Rena Mae, Juanita or Loretta.

Some teased their hair
into bouffant hairdos and
wore too much makeup.
Others wore outdated dresses and shoes,
and washed their hair with detergent soap.
They spoke in broken Indin-glish and
we used to laugh at them.

Joe Babes sat quietly
in the back of classrooms
even when they knew the answers,
were described as shy, dumb, angry, or on drugs
by the teachers.

These were the ones who stood in corners
for speaking Indian
until the government said it was okay.
Then they sang in Indian Clubs
and danced at pow-wows.
Joe Babes were given pernicious looks
by the cashier in the public school cafeteria

as they went through the line
because she thought they got free meals from the
government.

Joe Babes
laughed too loud

and were easily angered
when they got drunk.

Joe Babes
were the ones that left the reservations
for the cities, for the schools, for the jobs.

We were the Joe Babes.
All of us.

The Mane Story

Straight hair, black hair, brown hair, coarse hair, horse hair

We take turns ironing each other's hair. First Jenny. She kneels and I drape her black, thick, waist length, just washed, Prell-smelling hair onto the ironing board. I set the iron on rayon and press her hair flat into glossy satin ribbons. Suddenly her hair spills like a waterfall; it shimmers like corn tassels playing in the wind.

We know Lena for having the coarsest hair like horse hair. Bar none. Thick as the black bristles on the broom we use to sweep the steps leading into the front office. Lena's hair has a life of its own. It ignores the nightly green plastic rollers with which she tries to tame it.

Christie's hair falls below her waist. In the hallway she draws a paper warrior in colored charcoal on a roll of butcher paper for art class. When she leans forward, dark strands spill onto the drawing. The sound of her hair sweeping over paper is the sound of seeds tumbling inside a dry gourd.

Christianity Hopping

On Sunday mornings we were Presbyterian so we could drink coffee and eat Oreo cookies. Sunday evenings we were Christian Reformed because it was the farthest away from the dorm. You could get in a lot of hand holding and hugging on the way back if you had a boyfriend or girlfriend. Mormons don't drink coffee so we reserved Wednesday afternoons to be *Gáamalii,* Mormon. They let us slap dough into fry bread in the little kitchenette in the back as long as we cleaned up afterwards. The Catholics we stayed away from unless you were a member, because they looked threatening in their brown and white robes, and they were the last ones to let out on Sunday morning. *Éé'neishoodii,* Sweeping Robes, we called them. One Christmas we ventured there. If you skipped breakfast your stomach would be growling and making all kinds of embarrassing noises by then. They showed us a movie, Robin Hood or Zorro. Afterwards they gave us candy, nuts, apples and oranges in a green net bag. The hard candy stuck to the nuts in clumps and we gave it away or saved it till last. The apples were soft and spotted and the boys threw them at each other.

Once we even got on an old yellow church bus. On the freeway it chugged at fifty miles per hour top speed. Some of the boys who stayed behind teased us that our grandfather came all the way from Chinle to pick us up. Someone else added that it took a whole day for him to get just from Nine Mile Hill to the school. Another said our grandmother sat in the back of the bus while her *tsiiyéél,* hair bun, bobbed up and down. They joked that she ran alongside the bus and outraced it. We laughed imagining our old grandpa driving into a big city with grandma running in her long skirts and moccasins. Our grandpas and grandmas who might read and write only a little English, if any. Then one of the girls had the final word, *"Éí shįį nichai dóó nimásání t'ééya' ákódzaa."* "That's probably what your grandma and grandpa did." Yes, that's what we did, always running to stay caught up for the handouts.

One time Mary Lou and I wandered around in some church for almost an hour, looking at the quiet interior of finely carved mahogany banisters, stained glass windows, and rows of evenly spaced pews that sat in front of the podium. We went from room to room, looking, touching and sitting on the pews, turning the lights off and on, fingering the cold white keys on the organ, opening and closing the heavy gray velvet drapes. We looked in cupboards, opened drawers and refrigerator doors, smelled the inside of the oven, walked up and down thickly carpeted hallways, thumbed through songbooks, looked at framed pictures of bearded men in flowing robes, and then we got lost somewhere upstairs.

The Sacrament

One Sunday morning
after a spring rain
Mary Lou and I
went behind the Mormon church
on the corner of Cutler and Indian School Road.
There among the wet grass and soft brown earth
the air smelled heavy with
primordial smells of leaves, roots and water.

I don't remember who suggested it
but as if by some instinct
we scooped a handful of dirt
into our mouths.

It was like so many marbles
rolling and scattering
crunching between our teeth.

Later we sat in a neat row
    of metal folding chairs
    while the acne-faced Mormons
    broke up slices of white bread
    as we sang,
    ". . . as we eat the broken bread
    thine approval on us shed,
    as we drink the water clear. . . ."

Occasionally a grain or two of sand
                  still crunched in our mouths.

Popeye's Kitchen, a Letter from the Indian School II

Went to the Presbyterian church this morning. May Jean said they served coffee and cookies sometime. Sat through the services then went upstairs to the kitchen. The white women put Oreo cookies on the table and poured coffee. May Jean and I dunked our cookies and went back again and again until the women started giving us looks, you know, like they didn't want us doing it any more. We left for the dorm and waited an hour for the lunch bell to ring.

There's this man, the head cook, Popeye we call him, on account of he's a big, mean white man. Don't let you eat unless you do your detail. Stuff like serve food, clean trays, empty trash, wash heavy pans. You gotta report to the kitchen at 5:30 in the AM even on weekends, and that lasts for 9 weeks. Sometimes we fake being sick just to get out of it. Mostly he don't let the guys eat if they don't show up. Then somebody sneaks them rubber meat sandwiches or bear meat sandwiches, seeing as how we eat it four times a week.

The guys have to start reporting for their detail or eat when Popeye isn't in. There's Indian cooks too, mostly Pueblos and a Diné woman. Just keep washing those pots and don't mess with Popeye.

Woolworths

Went to Woolworths
down at the corner of Fourth and Central downtown
lots of skins hang out there
they call it the Indian Center
the bus stops out in front

Billie and I roamed among
record albums, make-up, hair spray
sprayed our hair platinum blonde
thought we'd get away from our straight black hair

you know, the Joe-Babe look

a clerk heard the hissing can and
ordered us to put it back or buy it
she watched us with eagle eyes

we ducked out of there
        and fled on the first bus back to the Indian School

Sometimes Those Pueblo Men Can Sure be Coyotes

Sometimes those Pueblo men can sure be coyotes
like the time Rena and I stayed late after school
we telephoned the Indian School to send
someone to pick us up

this time Mister Kayate drove up
in the gray "G-car," the government car
    that's what we called it
    and we had to call the men mister
    and the women missus
    but we students had other names for them
    because you know Diné easily make up names for people

so Rena and I got in the back
we were secretly pleased because we had
the best looking Pueblo man
chauffeuring us
at first we sat quietly
catching glimpses of his dark eyes in the rear view mirror
we had just pulled onto Central
when one of us said
    Éí hastiin ayóo baa dzólní' this man is very handsome
    Éí laa' I agree
then we were making all kinds of comments about him in Diné
our enthusiasm running away with us
saying those things adolescent girls say

    I wonder if he's married
    of course, these handsome men always have a woman
    how old do you think he is
    do you think he has children
                   and on and on

we did this
all the way back to the Indian School

not ever thinking he might understand us
until we got back
    A'héhee' at'ééke he said thank you, girls
as we half stumbled out of the car
our homework dropping on the sidewalk
that was the time a Pueblo coyote
chauffeured us in the "G-car"

Mennen Skin Bracer

Having a boyfriend meant holding hands at the movies
          in the dark auditorium,
someone besides your roommate to dance with,
and on Wednesday evenings having your name announced
over the intercom because he had walked across
          that brown grassy lot just to see you.

And you liked standing next to him until you casually
found each other's hand and how strong the bones felt.
Then you might remember what your mother said about
          "dropping him like a hot potato" if he turned out
to be your clan relative but you don't bring it up.

His name was Pierce and we worked kitchen detail.
I wasn't homely and I wasn't built
          like some of the others.
          I matured late.
                    "She looks smart" was what they said.
What did they know?
I was in culture shock for four years
          at the white public school
          and never made honorable mention.
Nobody was interested
          so I stopped trying.
Anyway Pierce asked me to dance Friday night.
Mostly we danced stomp, scooping and twirling to
                    The Wingate Valley Boys,
                    The Zuni Midnighters,
                    The Fenders,
you know, heavy on the bass.
Rah ja jin, rah ja jin.
So there I was on the floor
          nervous because it's my first time with a guy.
"Okay, I'm ready to show off my stuff," I thought.
All those months practicing with Mary Jean was paying off.

We went round and round.
He led me to the edge of the dance floor under the
                                          basketball hoop.
And all evening I smelled Mennen Skin Bracer.
Well, we danced a few more times and
afterwards Pierce walked me back to the dorm.
Later I found out he'd left a trail of broken hearts.
That evening the smell of Mennen Skin Bracer
lingered long on my hands.
And even now, when I'm in the grocery store
in the cosmetic department,
I'll open a bottle of Mennen Skin Bracer and take a whiff
of my first dance at the Indian School gym.

Dancing Boots

The screen door slams against the concrete wall of the house as I run out the door, down the sidewalk, and through the wooden gate. It flings against the branches of the Russian olives. I'm running as fast as I can down the dirt road towards the cattle guard that keeps the cows and horses out. I look back and see Davis gaining on me. The dust swirls in little clouds under our feet. Usually he chases me a little ways, stops, goes home and waits for his chance to pounce on me. This time he's intent on catching me. I fear another breath robbing punch in the stomach. Sometimes Gary is there to hit my breath back into me. Davis is closing in. I run faster, so does he. He grabs at my long hair as it flies behind me. I pull my hair around in front and keep running. I'm getting tired so I'm going to try something new. I stop suddenly, turn around and start running again. Davis keeps running. I can't help myself. It's hard to run and laugh at the same time. That's my mistake because it only makes him more angry. As laughter rolls through me, he grabs my wrists. I try to rotate my arms the way Len showed me. "When somebody grabs you by the wrists, just twist your hand under and that gets you out." But Davis's hold is too strong and I can't get out. We struggle and he twists my arm until the pain makes me cry. "I'll get you back," I yell as he runs off.

One Friday night, as we're doing the dishes, Davis and I hear the announcement over the radio that the Valley Boys are playing at the Armory. Davis snaps me with the dishtowel again which stings my arm and leaves a red mark. He says, "Hey, you want to go?" I'm looking at my arm and thinking of a way to get even. "I'll pay your way," he says which is his way of making up. After the last dish is put away, I slip on my stomp boots, the dishtowel sting forgotten temporarily. Davis teases me about my boots being my "dancing boots" because we live in town now. Mom must think it strange that her kids that fought the most now want to go to a dance together. We're on our way out the door when Mom tells Davis to watch out for me and to get home right away. I resent her overprotectiveness, after all I'm in high school now.

On the way to the Armory, I'm still thinking of a way to get even. Davis pays our admission, and we find ourselves in the gym with a few other couples and realize we're early. The band plays a fast number and the couples move to the center of the gym and slide and swing each other, classic Diné stomp dancing. The music stops and the couples move to the side again.

Another number begins and Davis asks a girl to stomp. In the meantime I'm the wallflower. I pretend nonchalance, like I'm waiting for a friend to arrive, so I look towards the doorway until the number ends. Davis returns and senses my dilemma. He stands next to me, and when the band begins the next number, he asks me to dance. He has a strong lead and we slide and swing all over the floor bumping into the other couples. They give us annoyed looks, but we keep right on dancing. He spins me around and around and I have a hard time keeping up with him. He slows down when he sees my rhythm isn't as fast as his. The number ends and we walk back to the sideline, my brother and I.

Visiting Cabbage Ears, a Letter from the Indian School III

Mae Jean showed me how to fake being sick. After the buses leave, you tell the matron you're sick and want to go to the clinic. She writes you a pass. At the clinic you go in and sit down with the other students. Pretty soon a Pinkie arrives, writes your name down on the clipboard and checks your pulse. She couldn't find my pulse, kept feeling all over my wrist. Then she tries the other side and the same thing happens. Pretty soon Mae Jean is laughing. The Pinkie gives her a dirty look and writes some numbers by my name. Then she takes our temperatures. Soon we're all sitting there with thermometers sticking out of our mouths, like one long pin cushion. When the Pinkie looks away, you rub the thermometer to warm it up so they'll think you have a fever. Jasper rubs his till the mercury shoots to the end and when it's his turn, we hear the doctor say if his temperature was that high he would've been dead by now. The next time we see Jasper, he looks like a dog with his tail tucked between his legs, sitting low in the G-car going down Cutler Road in the direction of school.

Mae Jean's turn comes and she goes behind the curtain where Cauliflower Ears, the doctor, asks her, "Do you have diarrhea?" You say yes so they'll believe you're really sick. "What color was it?" This is tricky because you have to remember the last time you had it so you can tell him. In the meantime the rest of us are listening and laughing. Soon Mae Jean reappears from behind the curtain with a red face and "Bed Rest" written on her pass. She gets to pretend being sick for one school day.

Then it's my turn to go behind the curtain to confront Cauliflower Ears. Somebody called him that and it stuck because his ears are the size of a cabbage leaf. Actually Cabbage Ears would've been a more appropriate name but what did we know about cauliflower, coming from a mutton and fry bread diet. Geez, this doctor looked older than salt. He must've retired at least three times from the army. He's old but still big and gnarly like a great big old tree that's been chopped down waiting for the trucks to pick it up. That was the PHS Indian School doctor who treated our "sickness" with bed rest and an envelope full of little white pills which we threw away as soon as we got back.

Covert Lover or How my *Na'ashshood* Days Ended

he was leading me behind the abandoned school buildings
one evening after supper
the gravel crackled under our steps
my thoughts heavy with anticipation
early stirrings of desires
when we got to the fire escape
sat down on the metal steps
leading down from the building
with the faded green paint beginning to peel away

he held my hand
I was thinking about that time
in the mountains
when we got away from the others
    that was the first time we kissed
        it was the end of the school year
            I knew I wasn't his first
                by the way he held me
    we stood a long time among the trees
        the scent of cedar
            the wind rustling down the mountains
                bending the trees
                    flowers playing in the wind
this time though
our meeting was meant to be covert
did I mention this was mid-September
and he was going to the State Fair
and needed money for rides and eats
this time of year we all were hoping for money from home
Pierce and I hadn't been together since
that time in the mountains

we sat there not saying anything
just listening to an occasional car drive by

outside the chain link fence that surrounded the school
he held my hand now
our thighs barely touching

then he asked if I had any money
and squeezed my hand
"a little"
"could you loan me four dollars?"
"why?"
"I'm going to the State Fair tomorrow"
I was peeling the paint now
and watching it fall
for awhile I might have
but this was a conspiracy
a stolen meeting
out of view
of the next girl in line
later I might have fought mad Mabel for him
because he jilted her for me
and she wanted to punch my lights out

when I told her she had better look
for the next girl
she settled down
and we became good friends
because we knew what it meant
to listen to the wind rustling
    and feel his breath
    and dared to hope for more
        somewhere in the mountains the wind was singing

So I Blow Smoke in Her Face

In the morning I race Łį́į'łitsoi across the open plain near the windmill. The prairie dogs must duck into their holes when they hear the thundering of hooves passing. My mother watches us from the doorway of the house as she mixes the dough for tortillas. The dust swirls behind us and she thinks I'm just like her mother was. People used to say she could ride: "That girl could ride bareback with her little brother sitting behind her and the dust swirling furiously behind them."

My family owns horses. Just west of Tohatchi is where I'm from. From the north window are the dark blue Chooshgai mountains rising above the dry plains and sand mesas on the southeast side. In the winter the Holy People emerge and cover the peaks with snow bringing us water for our spring fields. Sometimes I feel their breath blowing down the slopes and I know they are alive as a newborn colt steaming with life.

My uncle teases me because my legs are bowed. I wear tight Wrangler jeans so they show. My boots are creamy tan, the color of sand. The tips are dark brown and my boots are sexy.

In the summer we go by horseback to look for our cows. We take a sandwich and a canteen of water. We ride all morning moving south past sagebrush and green tumbleweeds towards Gallup looking for our brand on the right shoulders of our cows. I've memorized their spots and faces the way some people remember their addresses. When the sun moves overhead we ride west along the barbed wire fencing till we get to the bridge.

I like riding toward Chooshgai best, toward the cool mountain slopes. By midday we stop under the cottonwoods near the silver water tank and eat our potato and Spam tortilla sandwiches that Grandma packed. My cousin Viv and I scratch our initials into the water tank and when no one is looking I scratch in ER's initials.

We ride west toward the tall pine trees. On the way up we meet some riders who are also looking for their cattle and tell us they haven't seen our brand so we decide to turn around.

We stop at the trading post and tie the horses to an old elm tree. While Uncle waits, Viv and I go in and buy three Pepsis and a Payday. Uncle doesn't eat candy so Viv and I pass it back and forth until the leftover nuts roll around in the wrapper.

Viv and I race down the hill towards the highway. I pull my welder's hat down and give Łį́į'łitsoi free rein. The wind rushes past us. It flattens our faces and the earth cannot hold us. We are flying over sage, chamisa and the little yellow and purple flowers that spread across this broad land. I want to go on and on like this but the horses begin to foam at the mouth so we fall back into the horses and ride home slowly. They too know the exhilaration of a good run. Tonight I will give my horse extra oats and rub his back extra good with sand. Later, Uncle catches up and tells us we shouldn't tire the horses out like that. "Your mother won't like it," he adds to reinforce himself. My mother, the matriarch, is his older sister who inherited the homesite and most of the cattle and horses from her mother, as it is the Diné tradition for daughters to inherit the family's land and property.

It's late afternoon and the drifting clouds give us patches of shade. We ride slowly in the direction of home while Uncle sings riding songs to carry us back.

So I don't care if some of the girls have named me Wishbone. At least it's not as bad as the names the school has labeled me, troublemaker, incorrigible, dumb Indian. . . . One night they made me scrub the porches at midnight till my back ached. It's their way of shaming you, their way of taking control of you. They want you to know who's in charge, who's the authority. Like making soap flakes, they chip at you one flake at a time until your parts are laying in a bucket.

Then I light up a cigarette right there in the dorm. Soon the smoke drifts toward the ceiling like fog and the smell escapes from under the door and into the hallway, but I don't give anyone a chance to turn me in. I put on my jeans, navy blue sweatshirt, boots, and stuff my pockets with the last of the money from home.

On the way to Seven-Eleven I meet Viv who is usually willing to go along with my schemes. According to Diné kinship beliefs, we're sisters because our mothers are sisters. She's also my best friend. We've hauled water, scrubbed our clothes on a washboard down at the windmill, learned to make tortillas and even threw several batches of dough out into the brush behind the house because it was stiff as cold clay and we didn't want my mother to find out.

We walk across the campus, past the chain link fence ignoring the rules of signing in and out. Young pachucos in their low riders whistle at us. Usually we ignore them, preferring cowboys and their music. But tonight I want the company of wildness. So we enter their car and cruise up and down Central, two stomp Diné girls and two Chicanos. We laugh and laugh until they get serious. We drive down Fourth and I tell the driver to let us out. They don't want to but when I tell them we're government property and they could get into a lot of trouble, the door swings open.

The sun is sinking behind the treetops when I think of Edgar. I tell Viv let's cut across the houses toward Tanoan Hall. We make it back as the last of the students are coming from dining room detail. We walk to Edgar's window which is the fourth one down from the end, and look through the steel mesh that covers all the windows that were installed after the dorm attendants found students crawling out at night after bedcheck to visit girlfriends in other dorms or to go to Seven-Eleven.

"Shhhhd, Edgar." We give the Diné signal. Someone jumps off the bunkbed and sees us. He pulls the curtain back. It's Jasper, Edgar's cousin. "Oh, hi Jasper. Edgar *hágo bidiní.*" He leaves and brings Edgar. Edgar smiles at me from behind the mesh cover and says "cigarette-*ísh nee hóló?*" I pull out a pack of Winstons from my boot and we light up and exhale streams of smoke.

"Is it time for your bedcheck?" I tease. It's just an expression that we use to make a joke. Just something to laugh about, living in these government boarding schools. The practice of making sure everyone is in bed at 10:00 is another carryover from military life that these schools are modeled after. Edgar blows a cloud of smoke through the steel mesh and shows me his hands.

"I have dishpan hands," he announces and puts his fingers through the mesh to show us. Sure enough, the finger tips are shriveled and the nails are soft and pale. His fingers are those of a Diné, long, slender, thin-skinned and brown. Some people notice faces but I notice hands. It was in the kitchen as he gathered trays to scrub that I first saw his hands. "I just got back from kitchen detail. They're so clean I could operate with them," he jokes and stares at his hands.

"*Hát'íílá naadeidą́ą́?* Was it bear meat again?*Viv asks. It's a joke because it's at least three or four times a week that we have salisbury steak or roast beef, otherwise known as bear meat and rubber meat, respectively. The rubber meat could pass for beef jerky, seeing how all the moisture is cooked out of it.

Car lights pass down the street outside the fence, and I remember my family going to Chooshgai to gather wood in the fall. From the mountain top we can see a thin line of car lights moving across the plain in the far distance below. It made me feel better, just thinking about cutting and piling wood into my dad's truck, and how Grandma would boil coffee and cook us mutton stew so that by the time we had finished stacking the last log, the meal would be ready. I knew Viv and I shouldn't be here at Edgar's window, but sometimes you just have to take control of your life and not let someone take it away from you. At home Viv and I took care of the cows the way Mom showed us, because most of the herd was hers. She taught us how to herd, how to vaccinate, how to rope and throw down the calves at branding time, and how to take care of our cattle. I had never gotten a summer job working as a clerical aid for the community or the chapter house the way others my age did. Taking care of my family's cattle was my responsibility when I was at home. Because I cared for the cows, Mom had given me a few of hers. I even had my own brand.

"Nihíma nicháa'ha'dooshkeeł." Edgar teases back. He jokes about Mrs. Harry, who is the head matron, and if she catches us will give us extra detail or ground us. On campus she has a reputation for being a mean woman even though she's an Indian, a Heinz 57, an Indian who's from several different tribes.

" *'Éí laa'*. She's had it in for me ever since I got back late from Christmas vacation," I say as I inhale. Mrs. Harry, the woman who on my first day at the Indian School made everyone scurry away from the rear exit and back to their beds when they saw her car rounding the corner, breeds fear in the hearts and minds of the girls in my dorm. They avoid making her angry because she'll make you scrub, sweep, or clean something even for minor infractions. She's always trying to catch me breaking the rules, and sometimes she makes me do extra work around the dorm if she sees me talking in the hallway, like the time she told me to mop up the water in the showers when it wasn't my detail, or the time she told me to sweep the porch after Edgar walked me back from the rec hall. "No sweeping, no TV," she said. I said okay and went into my room. Ever since then she watches my every move.

Mrs. Chavez, the girl's dorm attendant, sees us at Edgar's window as she makes her rounds and tells us to get back to our dorm. "Mrs. Harry wants to see you, Vida" she says and looks at me.

"Another month in the salt mines," I say sarcastically and stomp out the cigarette. It leaves a black smear on the concrete.

I'm lying on my bunk bed and thinking about home. I'm thinking about the calves nuzzling their mothers. I'm thinking about Łįį'łitsoi and riding him across the dry plains, under the bridge and towards the Chooshgai. I'm thinking about tall straight pine trees and the cool breeze that drifts from the mountain. I'm thinking about the smell of sage after a summer rain. I'm thinking of mom's warm, round tortillas.

Viv sits beside me and dangles her feet from the top of my bunkbed. We take turns smoking my cigarette. Then there's the knock at the door and sure enough she has sent Apple Annie, her favorite, to get me. Viv and I exchange looks. I step out into the hallway by the bulletin board, where my name has often appeared with the other offenders. She's waiting there with hand on hip. The other girls are watching from their rooms, as if this were a showdown. She's ready to tell me off, to shame and humiliate me again. But I don't give her a chance, so I take a drag and blow smoke in her face.

Yes, my mother thinks, my daughter is just like her grandmother, as she watches me riding outside the northwest fence where the cows graze. She returns to her weaving. The design grows upward in layers of dramatic and geometric shapes.

Łįį'łitsoi and I move easily through the trees. We've been this way before. He picks his way steadily up the mountain slopes. The clean mountain air feels good. My horse is strong and happily we make the climb up the Chooshgai.

Collage

JB,
Well—you've
asked for one
of these ugly
looking "pics."
Don't let it
scare you away.
    Lots of luck
in everything
you undertake.
    Always me,
    Doughnut

To JB,
    Gee! It's been great to
have you as a pal
again. Wish we could
be roommates again.
Always remember your
education comes first.
May God Bless You.
    Always your pal,
    Virgie

JB,
    You're a real
pretty chick with the
biggest personality
to grab anyone.
I hope we
have fun with
universities.
    Billie

JB,
    To the best
rider on this side of
Rio Grande. You are
very nice to know as a
cousin and I am glad I
have you as cousin.
May God Bless You and
good luck in the future.
    Winnie T.

JB,
Just a photo
to recall our
"soph" year.
Stay sweet.
    Carilene

To JB,
You are a very
nice friend, so just
keep it up. This is
just for you to
remember me by.
    Mae Jean

Part II

No Parole Today

conversations in passing

two university vans!
man, if that wasn't letting
all the animals out of the zoo
we were on our way to seattle for the niea
when we got to brigham city
it was wake up man!
got any brothers or sisters or cousins in intermountain?
we need a place to crash
it was party all the way!
i mean make-out city   pow-wow all night
49 to the max! and snagging!
that was some trip
that was when larry was still alive   you remember larry
larry casuse?
he kidnapped the mayor of gallup   him and bob
held him hostage
right there at that sporting goods store on highway 66
you know   that main street where all the tourists
pass through on their way to california
that's the street where all the winos get picked up
and put in jail
        sheeeit!   what they call pc
        protective custody
        they put my brother in there all the time
        i'm telling you
        that ain't no protective custody
        three times they beat him up
        once they broke his arm
        and cracked a rib
        wouldn't even take him to the hospital

damn!   you know he used to be in special forces
went to nam even
guess he tried to use that fightin' stuff he learned
but there were too many cops   sticks and feet

when he came back from nam all he could do was drink
now he spends a lot of time in and out
of the va hospital
he ain't getting any better
nobody knows what to do for him anymore

so like i was telling you about larry
he had this crazy idea that he could stop the system
so he and bob took the mayor out of city hall
and marched him at gunpoint down to the
sporting goods store
said he was gonna show the world what a false person he was
that's what he called him   false person
see larry found out this mayor guy was just appointed
to the board of regents
not only that he was also part owner of the navajo inn
that liquor store just outside the rez near window rock
that place where probably hundreds of skins got wiped out
    in the bushes   on the roads   in the ditch
    helpless kids crying and clinging
    to their moms' skirts
    dads gone astray on the weekend
    teenagers out to party then getting into wrecks
    grandmas and grandpas that never made it home

talk about massacre   that place was another sand creek
only this time the killers came in liquid form
larry never had a chance
during the shoot-out
larry got killed
of course   the police said it was self-inflicted
i mean they run the whole town, most of it anyway

so it's been ten years now since that ordeal
maybe we'll survive the streets of that town

My Brother Shakes the Bottle

Davis is wearing his best irrelevant boots and jacket.
It's been at least a month that he's owned them.
He looks twenty years older than I
though we're only a year apart.
The faces tell us
what we already know from the bordertowns
about being waited on last even though
we were in line first.

Davis orders what I do.
He tries not to make waves,
not to make demands.
So he stutters to the adolescent waitress,
"Can I have some sweet'n low"?

On the other side of the counter,
under the fluorescent lights, sits a local
wearing a SEED cap.
Between bites, he watches us.
These faces are clues
to what drove my brother to slump on that red ant hill
in the Arizona desert
where only the sagebrush and rabbits
must have felt the earth shake a little.

In their eyes
I see the night, when anything can happen.
It is then in his room at the VA
my brother shakes the bottle
that explodes
all over
himself.

Body Identified

That Thursday afternoon when I
was getting dressed for work,
the newspaper landed with a dull thud on the steps.
It must have
kicked up the dust a little.
And as I combed out my hair, my mom
came across the paragraph:
"Young male Indian
in the early 20s found alongside the highway near Twin
Lakes."

My God, it was on a Greyhound bus in Durango
that I first told you I loved you.
The girl who sat behind us must've heard me make such bold
confessions
through the space between the seats.
Then in silence I fell asleep on your lap.
You must've watched me
dream the La Plata Mountains alone.
The words I uttered weren't enough to keep you.
The nights we clung together
rejected us
and now your life had erupted all over the highway.
In April
you came to pick up that black and white sweater from my
closet.

After the services
I remember wanting to swerve off the highway and into the
sagebrush.
You died for me
one June summer day
in one paragraph of the newspaper.

Newspaper Deaths

I can flip my life back to the page
    when you showed up at midnight   drunk

When we stayed all night in the backseat at Church Rock
When you sent me a poster of Alcatraz Island
When I found you hidden in a tiny column of the newspaper

You played with your soul
how he deserted you next to Highway 666
    and nobody   nobody   would touch you
Diné have always been afraid of death
They must have looked down at you with fearful eyes

Were you lonely?
Were you afraid?
Did you think of cars running over you?
Did you think of me?

You sent me no letter, no telephone call, no note
Just that lousy clipping I never saved
And the police just added another number to their records

The Shooting

Sarah T's husband shot her at the Tohatchi laundromat
while she unloaded the quilts from the pickup truck

he waited for her in an arroyo across the highway
under the Russian olives
then took careful aim

she fell back
the laundry scattered at her feet

and the blood steamed red
all over the rocks

Sarah T's husband waited until the ambulance had gone
then pulled the last bullet on himself in a half-moon light

He said he didn't want to go alone

No Parole Today

*In 1980 prisoners rioted in the Santa Fe State prison. After several days
of violence and bloodshed, the prison was retaken by the authorities.*

A shadow of smoke passed
over my dreams
I awoke trying to remember what was said
about Santa Fe and prison
the blood and emotions spilling over
I dressed and poured a cup of coffee

      then I remembered

my own scars
lying on bunk beds
and listening to
floor polishers whirling
and the bell that drove me
to sneaking behind cars and freeways

I swore then I would never
scrub no more walls
and porches at midnight
not for the woman
who sits sideways in auditorium chairs
and steals bacon from the back door
as easily as she could steal your confidence
I'm not from here
no more rubber meat and showering on cement floors
I learned early that my life
was separated by walls
and roll calls

Last night they said
a thousand men uncapped themselves behind barbed wire and smoke

Sometimes She Dreams

This woman
I call my mother
quit school in her teens to follow
                    her Grand Canyon dreams
                    where she dreams of becoming
more than maid, waitress, cook, wife.

As the bus races down the smooth highway
the magazine falls open on her lap and she fills
in her name on the white card
                    to the "LaSalle Extension School of Law—
            Learn law at home in your spare time."
But she never sends it.

Through the shiny reflection of the glass window
she sees the wooden billboards along Highway 66 near Lupton,
"See Real Indians Inside Making Jewelry, Weaving Rugs."

This isn't what her mother wanted
but she seems destined to follow the same highway
her mother took to a kitchen in California
where the dishes rattled in their cupboards.
The bus stops in front of the big hotel
where she later stripped and tightened the bed covers
after the tourists left.
And outside the Canyon stretched wide her arms
                    the way her dreams must have felt
                    back then,
                    wide and open,
                            so much space to be filled.

Little Sister

for Frank LaMere

In 1984 the body of twenty-one year old Michelle LaMere from Winnebago, Nebraska, was found in north Omaha where she had been run over by a car.

I was the youngest of nine children. The morning they found me, the mulberries had already given away their young fruit. And summer was a smooth, slender, dark woman dancing to the center of the drum. My grandfathers' voices still rise above the rolling hills along the Niobrara where my people dance.

But my voice was invisible against the onslaught. Their words lie. They create divisions, arrange my life in numbers, add and subtract me and put me into neat boxes for storage.

My life unraveled early alone in a large city where I followed shadows and chased the jagged promise of empty bottles. There I thought I heard my father's voice softly calling me "Baby, baby, you're my baby" when my mother first unwrapped me, a newborn present, a young heartbeat to strengthen the drum.

In the blossoming light the earth goes on gathering the dripping fruit of mulberries in her outstretched arms along the Niobrara. In the season of gathering mulberries I danced the fury of buffalo and dreamed the slender, dark woman and my brother singing, singing in the voice of praise:

Little sister, little sister,
tasted her life again
in the spiraling dance of thunder beings,
and buffalo
and was borne away in the
thunderclouds
and the rain that
fell and fell
afterwards.

Half-Light

My son and I sat on the bed of a late half-light
from the hallway slanted across gray walls.

He spoke of toes and scratches,
and I comforted in the desert tones of our language
we left behind across winter dry plains.

His brown eyes
alive,
    glowing in the shadows with eternal life,
gaze at me,
feeling the sounds of these words
I so seldom speak.

In this moment caught between languages
    we shared my words
        as if they were secrets
nourished within this half-light.

Oil

To those who put rocks behind bars

Imagine all the dinosaurs underground that turned into oil. How long does it take to make oil? And while we're on the subject are the dead in their coffins turned into oil by now? What if all the coffins contained puddles of oil? Imagine all that oil gone to waste. How long does it take to turn oil into gas? What if you could siphon gasoline out of the coffins? Would people drive up with empty tanks to the cemetery? Would the relatives will their oil to their future generations? Would there be signs outside the graveyards advertising who was leaded and unleaded? Would Orson Welles be considered diesel fuel? Would Lawrence Olivier be considered regular? How many coffins would it take to fill a gas tank? Would undertakers become oil brokers? Would coffins be manufactured with gas nozzles on the lids? Could we get nachos and rent movies at the graveyard station? When a car drives into the cemetery will a bell ring?

When the Moon Died

Peter McDonald, former President of the Diné Nation, was convicted of various illegal activities and is now serving a prison sentence.

When the moon died
we watched in silent awe
the closing of her light
above the treetops.

> My father's voice comes back to me:
>   "It's a bad sign for us
>   when it happens at night.
> It hasn't rained here,"
>   and we look eastward
>   at the thirsty earth,
> the sun bearing down
>   on the cracks in the ground.
> "We must not be living right."

The neighbor brought out a
camera and aimed it
at the moon.
Minutes later only a
blurred image emerged.

> "If it happens during the day,
>   it's bad for the white people.
> Years ago the flu killed a lot
>   of them.
> It was bad."

I returned to the typewriter while
the moon hid herself
as if in shame.

> "They say you're not supposed
>   to do anything,

don't go to bed,
don't eat. Pregnant
    women shouldn't see it.
Three people shot because of
    McDonald.
We're not living right."

When the moon died
she reminded us of
the earth ripping apart
violent tremors,
greasy oceans,
the panic of steel winds,
whipping shorelines and
thirsty fields.
Grandfather trees pulled
for profit.
The Earth is angry at the people.
We're not living right.

Easter Sunday

Driving to the mountains at noon
    through sagebrush and pinon trees
children gather wood   uncle builds fire
    mother and daughters prepare food

flames burning good and hot
    coals ready   grill on   push coals around

stew on   stir it now and then
    skillet ready for fry bread   watch smoke rise
    slap dough into large thin circles   edges lumpy
    pull dough   make holes   it's okay
    put in skillet anyway   watch it floating
    makes bubbles   turns brown   turn it over
    feel heat on face and hands

Grandma scolding Aunt   doesn't know how
    to cut mutton ribs   Grandma fixes   put back
    on grill   watch ribs sizzle brown   turn over
    drop in ashes   dust it off   put back on grill
    hope Grandma didn't see

Fry bread stack getting higher
    push more coals under skillet
    my son moves closer to the fire   raises hand
    "hot hot" he says   uncle comes
    takes him away   from cooking

stew boiling over   hisses and drips into the coals
    take lid off   coffee steaming
    grounds bubbling
    breeze blowing   carries away coffee smell

Ribs cooked   coffee boiled   fry bread stacked
stew boiled   stomach grumbling   mouth watery
anticipation

plates full   sit down   under tree
family together

               give thanks

                        we eat now.

At Mexican Springs

Up here I can see the
    glimmering lights of Gallup calling the
        reservation
    like a whore standing under a light post
    the way they do in Juarez
    in Gallup   when our sons are born they say
    "she gave birth to a wino"
    Gallup steals our children
    returns them empty and crumbled

But here the hills are quietly breathing
    the earth is a warm glowing blanket
    holding me in her arms
        It is here among the sunset in
            every plant
            every rock
            every shadow
            every movement
            every thing

        I relive visions of ancient stories
            First Woman and First Man
            their children stretched across
            these eternal sandstones
            a deep breath
            she brings me sustenance
            life
    and I will live to tell my children these things.